Wombat Tour Guide!

Wombat Books would like to acknowledge the Traditional Owners of the land on which we visit in *Around Australia in 30 Places*. We wish to pay respect to their Elders—past, present and emerging—and acknowledge the important role Aboriginal and Torres Strait Islander people continue to play within the communities of the places we are about to visit.

Attention! Attention! Calling all young adventurers.

Come with me as I take you on a quick trip around Australia in 30 places. Some places you may know, but there's always somewhere new to discover! From vast plains of red sand to the white shells of the Opera House, there's so much to explore.

Are you ready?

Around Australia in 30 Places

© Wombat Books, 2020
© Rochelle Manners , 2020

Published by Wombat Books, 2020
P.O. Box 1519, Capalaba, QLD 4157
www.wombatbooks.com.au
info@wombatbooks.com.au

ISBN: 978-1925563757

A catalogue record for this
book is available from the
National Library of Australia

Evie Larcombe

Samantha Parish

30. Rise and shine! Let's start our trip with the Sunshine State in Brisbane. It's home to Australia's only beach in the middle of a city. Dip your toes in the water while looking out at tall skyscrapers.

Brisbane, QLD

29. Slop some sunscreen on for a beach trip to Coolangatta. We're now at the entrance to Queensland's Gold Coast, where—believe it or not—the sands are golden! You might even have the time to loop-de-loop on a roller coaster at one of the many theme parks here.

Coolangatta, QLD

(Amber) Yuxuan Liang

28. Stanthorpe is a quaint Queensland town, boasting delicious apple pies. I hear along the grapevine that it has a lot of vineyards. Make sure you bring a jumper as the town can get an occasional winter snowfall!

Stanthorpe, QLD

Lara Winton

27. Inverell is known as the Sapphire City with its production of precious stones. However, with lakes for fishing and picturesque views, you're sure to find a few more hidden gems.

Inverell, NSW

6

THE BIG BANANA COFFS HARBOUR

Rebecca Tang

26. On our way to Sydney, we'll stop off at Coffs Harbour. At this home of the Big Banana, you're sure to find many tasty, real bananas too.

A place with beautiful views and a bunch of things for the family to do.

Coffs Harbour, NSW

7

Berylia Nuraina

25. Spotted: The Sydney Harbour Bridge. It's a bit of a climb but well worth the views of Australia's largest city, Sydney. Over there is the Opera House, where you can catch a concerto, and over there is Taronga Zoo, where you're sure to spot a roo.

Sydney, NSW

Caitlin Miller

24. We're travelling through the Blue Mountains now. See those stones towering over the range? They're the Three Sisters from an Indigenous Australian Dreaming story. At the foothill of the mountains is the world's oldest known cave system, the Jenolan Caves. Don't get caught in the Dragon's Throat!

Blue Mountains, NSW

Aramis Surtees

23. Phew! We've reached our capital city of Canberra. Make sure you visit the Parliament House, Australian War Memorial and National Library of Australia. You can even take a cruise along an artificial lake—Lake Burley Griffin. Don't worry, it's real water!

Canberra, ACT

Sonya Clarke

22. We'll stop in Wagga Wagga just in time to cheer on the rafters competing in the town's famous Gumi Race! Look at them drifting down the Murrumbidgee River in their rubber vessels—don't get splashed as they pass us!

Wagga Wagga, NSW

11

Blake Ellerman

21. There's something fishy about Fish Creek—and it might have something to do with all the fish around town. There's a giant mullet on top of the local hotel and fish-shaped seats all around.

Fish Creek, VIC

12

Luna Park

Jack Morris

20. We've reached the hub of Australian arts and culture: Melbourne City. Walk down alleyways filled with colourful graffiti, try international cuisines, see live bands, catch a musical and don't forget to visit the Queen Victoria Market!

Melbourne, VIC

Zach Searle

19. Let's stop over for the penguin parade at Phillip Island. Watch thousands of little penguins—the smallest species of penguin—waddle up the beach to their homes in the sand dune burrows while the sun fades behind the sea.

Phillip Island, VIC

HOBART NATIONAL PARK

Ella Zieserl

18. We'll have to catch a boat down to Tasmania, our Australian island friend. It's filled with unique wildlife, including the Tasmanian Devil and lush national parks. From Hobart, we'll go Aurora chasing to see what is known as the Southern Lights.

Hobart, TAS

Belle Ritchie

17. If you venture too far while you're down here, you might find yourself at the Edge of the World! You'll be looking at the longest uninterrupted section of ocean on the planet. It might get a bit windy!

Edge of the World, TAS

Ruby Wandschneider

16. We're at King Island now, so take a deep breath in because it's some of the cleanest air in the world. From a lighthouse to offshore shipwrecks, it's a peaceful piece of land to explore. You may even have time for some fish and chips.

King Island, TAS

Abbey Olafsen

15. Check out Sovereign Hill, as it's pure gold to visit! Seriously, it has a replica Gold Rush town. Learn about Australia's goldfields from costumed ladies and gents. You can even try panning for your own fortune!

Ballarat, VIC

18

Rory Smith

14. Let's wind down along the Great Ocean Road.
You are sure to get some wonderful photographs of beaches
as you twist and curve around the long coastal road.

Watch the sunset over the Twelve Apostles—
majestic rocks that rise from the ocean.

Great Ocean Road, VIC

13. Shh … we'll be quiet as we explore the underground limestone caves at Naracoorte. Look at the fossilised remains of thousands of animals. We'll try and avoid the bats but there's no guarantee … best to try to keep quiet.

Naracoorte, SA

Teniel Sauer

Andrew Philip

12. In Adelaide, I've got the cricket bats ready! Australians love their cricket, so make sure to check out Adelaide Oval and pose with the Donald Bradman statue. Want to whisper me a secret across the Whispering Wall? Your voice will travel to me from over 100 metres away!

Adelaide, SA

Anna Rose Gray

11. Ready! Set! Go! The camels are off on a race in the Flinders Ranges. Nearby is the historic Dog Fence, built to keep the dingoes away from crops and sheep. It's fairly hot here, so I hope you brought a hat!

The Flinders Ranges, SA

NEXT 90 km

Daisy Karner

10. Australia is a land of lush rainforests and sunny beaches, but also flat, endless countryside. Welcome to the Nullarbor Plain—one never-ending stretch of treeless, arid desert. Crossing the Nullarbor along the Eyre Highway will take you some time, but it is an unmissable road trip experience.

Nullarbor Plain, WA

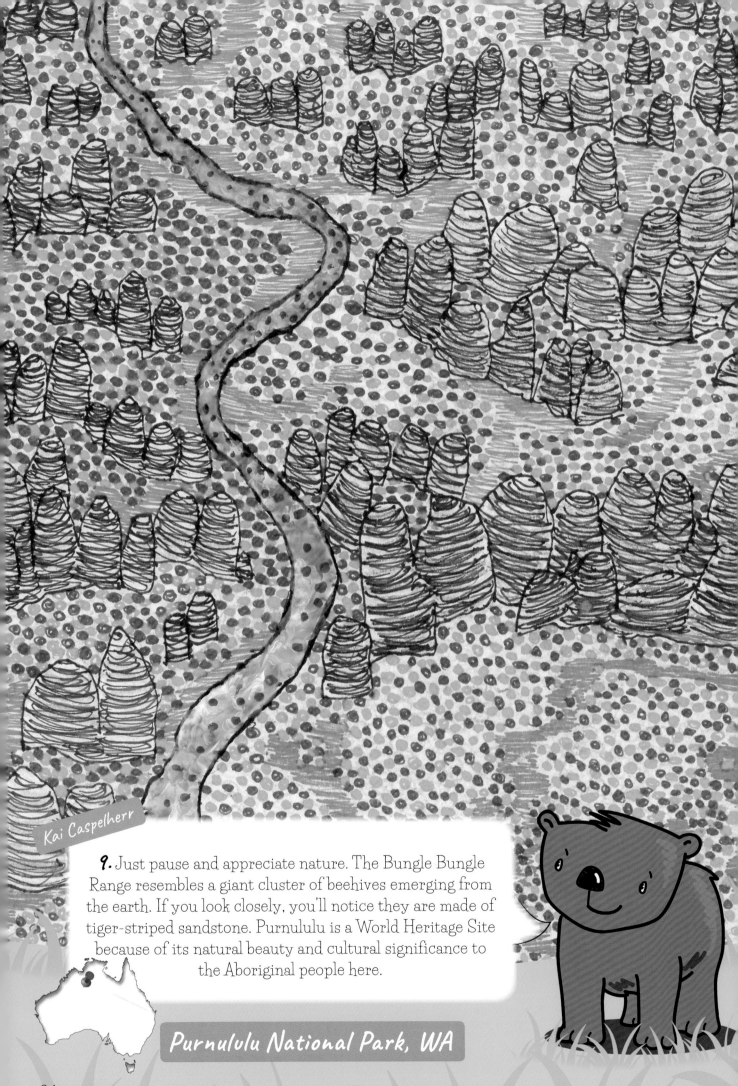

Kai Caspelherr

9. Just pause and appreciate nature. The Bungle Bungle Range resembles a giant cluster of beehives emerging from the earth. If you look closely, you'll notice they are made of tiger-striped sandstone. Purnululu is a World Heritage Site because of its natural beauty and cultural significance to the Aboriginal people here.

Purnululu National Park, WA

Alexey Luchkovskiy

8. We've reached the jewel of the Kimberley: Lake Argyle, the second largest man-made reservoir in Australia. Watch out for the freshwater crocodiles—there are over 35,000 of them ... which is more than the number of people in this region!

Lake Argyle, WA

Lara Tamke

7. It's time for a swim at Kakadu. You might even glimpse Namarrgon, the Lightning Man, in the ancient gallery of rock paintings. These rocks have been a canvas for Indigenous stories for thousands of years.

Kakadu, NT

Nathan Kingsley

6. We're at the heart of Australia: Uluru. The Red Centre. It's a sacred connection to the land for the Yankunytjatjara and Pitjantjatjara people. Uluru never remains the exact same colour but changes each day with the light and atmosphere ... so make sure to get lots of snaps!

Uluru, NT

Scarlett Papps-Burford

5. You may need to swat some flies out here in Alice Springs. Drop into the School of the Air Visitor Centre; they have the world's largest classroom. If you're lucky, you might also catch the Henley-On-Todd Regatta, a 'boat' race on a dry riverbed.

Alice Springs, NT

Ruby Levitt

4. Snorkels out! We can't miss Australia's iconic natural wonder: The Great Barrier Reef.

It's the world's largest coral reef and the only living thing that is visible from space.

The Great Barrier Reef, QLD

Layla Gill

3. With over 300 islands, the Torres Strait is Australia's most northern point. It was regularly bombed in WWII but remains a virtually untouched natural environment.

The Torres Strait Islands are home to one of the oldest continuing living cultures on Earth.

Torres Strait Islands, QLD

Britney Fallon

2. Rockhampton is best known for its beef cattle. There are six bull statues around town—one for each breed in the region. But don't be surprised if other life-size bull statues pop up—residents create them for competitions!

This is also one of the best places in Australia to check out a rodeo.

Rockhampton, QLD

Tommy Clements

1. The last stop is my home of Capalaba. The name Capalaba comes from a Yugarabul word for 'ring-tailed scrub possum', and I do have a lot of possum friends here.

My cosy burrow is waiting for me. Have a safe trip to wherever in Australia you call home.

Redlands, QLD